No previous knowledge of the recorder or music is needed
in order to begin playing with this specially written recorder
course for 7-11 year olds.

The **Pupil's Books** are carefully graded with clear explanations
at every stage, encouraging children to develop musical skills as
well as recorder techniques.

A **Cassette** for each stage provides models for children to copy
and interesting accompaniments to encourage enjoyable practice
and performance.

Tune Books contain extra graded tunes and duets to help pupils
to consolidate their skills at each level.

The **Teacher's Books**, one for each stage, include simple piano
accompaniments, guitar chord symbols and suggestions for playing
each tune in the pupil's books.

This series comprises the following books and cassettes:

Pupil's Book 1 EJ10006 ISBN 0-7119-5079-2
Pupil's Book 2 EJ10007 ISBN 0-7119-5080-6
Pupil's Book 3 EJ10008 ISBN 0-7119-5081-4

Cassette 1 EJ10009
Cassette 2 EJ10010
Cassette 3 EJ10011

Tune Book 1 EJ10000 ISBN 0-7119-5073-3
Tune Book 2 EJ10001 ISBN 0-7119-5074-1
Tune Book 3 EJ10002 ISBN 0-7119-5075-X

Teacher's Book 1 EJ10012 ISBN 0-7119-5085-7
Teacher's Book 2 EJ10042 ISBN 0-7119-5114-4
Teacher's Book 3 EJ10014 ISBN 0-7119-5086-5

Treble Recorder From The Beginning EJ10003 ISBN 0-7119-5076-8
Treble Recorder From The Beginning Teacher's Book EJ10004 ISBN 0-7119-5077-6

EJA Publications
Order No.EJ10007

ISBN 0-7119-5080-6

KU-041-826

9 780711 950801

Class Activities

There are special opportunities for recorders to join with **singers**, and others playing easy-to-learn **ostinati** on xylophones and other instruments on these pages:

page 3	London's burning	Singers	xylophone/chime bar ostinato
page 20	Little Red Wagon/ Skip to my Lou	Singers	
page 26	Kookaburra	Singers	xylophone/chime bar ostinato
page 31	Row, Row, Row your boat	Singers	xylophone/chime bar ostinato
page 38	Hollow elm tree	Singers	
page 39	Li'l Liza Jane	Singers	xylophone/chime bar ostinati
page 43	I like the flowers	Singers	xylophone/chime bar ostinati

The Teacher's Book includes many other percussion accompaniments to play along with the recorder parts.

Recorder *from the* Beginning

Book 2

John Pitts

This recorder course in 3 stages has been designed for children aged 7 upwards. Since publication it has become one of the most popular schemes used in many parts of the world. **Recorder from the Beginning** assumes no previous knowledge of either music or the recorder, and full explanations are provided at every stage so that specialist teaching is not essential. Teacher's Books are available for each stage, and these contain simple piano accompaniments, guitar chord symbols and suggestions for each tune.

Cassette tapes of accompaniments are now available, in response to popular demand. These include a model version of each tune, followed by exciting rhythmic accompaniments for recorders to play along with, both in school and at home.

The new coloured edition of the books has allowed more emphasis on activities directly related to aspects of Music in the National Curriculum. For example, opportunities are provided for recorder players to be accompanied by instrumental ostinati and other percussion accompaniments and for recorders to perform with singers in two-part items, rounds, songs with descants and other activities.

John Pitts 1993

Acknowledgements

The publishers would like to thank the following for permission to include their copyright material: Workers' Music Association, the melody of *The Fireman's not for me* from *the Shuttle and Cage* (Ewan MacColl); Jan Holdstock, the words and music of *Down in Bethlehem*.
The music on the following pages has been specially composed and arranged for this book by the author: 2, 8, 17, 19 (bottom), 23 (bottom), 27, 29 (bottom), 31 (top), 34, 35, 40 (bottom), 45, 47.

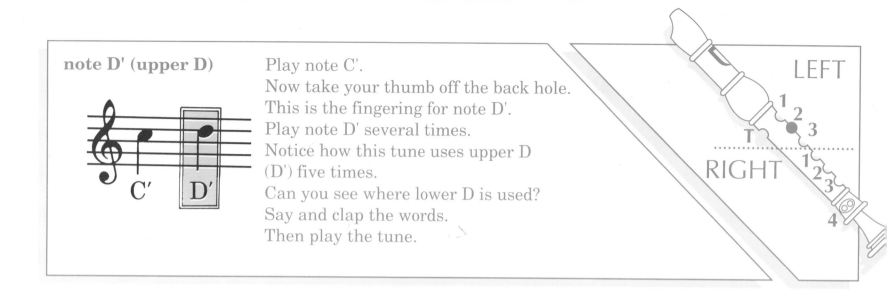

note D' (upper D)

C' D'

Play note C'.
Now take your thumb off the back hole.
This is the fingering for note D'.
Play note D' several times.
Notice how this tune uses upper D
(D') five times.
Can you see where lower D is used?
Say and clap the words.
Then play the tune.

LEFT

RIGHT

Way down South

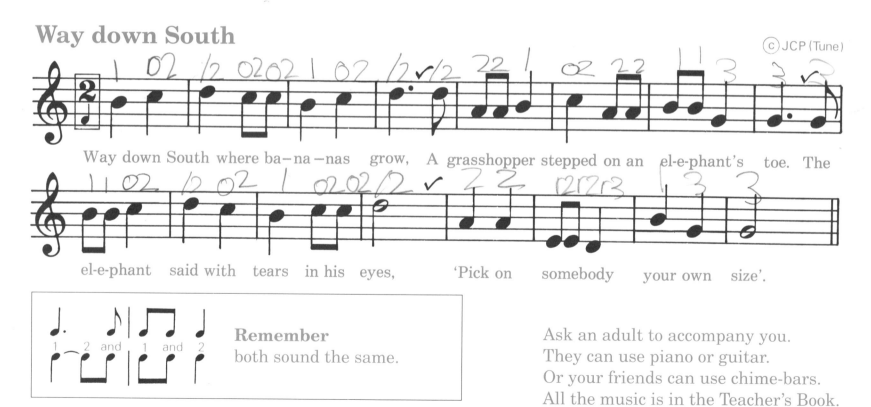

Way down South where ba–na–nas grow, A grasshopper stepped on an el-e-phant's toe. The

el-e-phant said with tears in his eyes, 'Pick on somebody your own size'.

Remember
both sound the same.

Ask an adult to accompany you.
They can use piano or guitar.
Or your friends can use chime-bars.
All the music is in the Teacher's Book.

2

Ten in the bed

This tune begins with the end of a bar. To begin, count 1–2–3 and play on count 4.

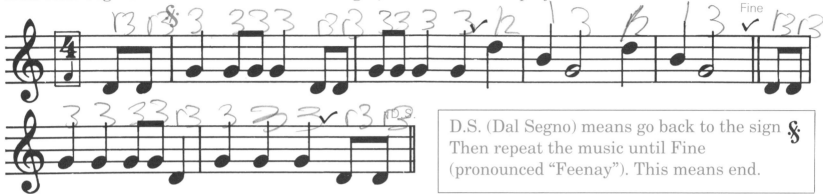

D.S. (Dal Segno) means go back to the sign 𝄋
Then repeat the music until Fine
(pronounced "Feenay"). This means end.

London's burning   Count 1–2 and play on count 3.

Lon‑don's bur‑ning   Lon‑don's bur‑ning   Fetch the   en—gines ,   fetch the   en‑gines , Fire,

fire ——— !   Fire,   fire ——— !   Pour on   wa—ter ,   Pour on   wa—ter .

Class Activity

When you know this tune well, you can play it as a **Round** in 2, 3 or 4 parts. Or some **Singers** can be Group 1 (and 3) with Recorders as Group 2 (and 4).

Ostinato accompaniment. You can use the first or last phrase of the round as an ostinato accompaniment (repeating pattern). Play it on xylophone or chime bars. Let the ostinato begin first before the singers and recorders join in with the round. Later try both ostinati together.

Amazing Grace
Remember to tongue–slur where a curved line joins **different** notes (slurred).

A —ma——zing grace, how sweet the sound, That saved a wretch like me——. I
once—— was lost, but now—— I'm found, Was blind, but now I see——.

Over the sea to Skye

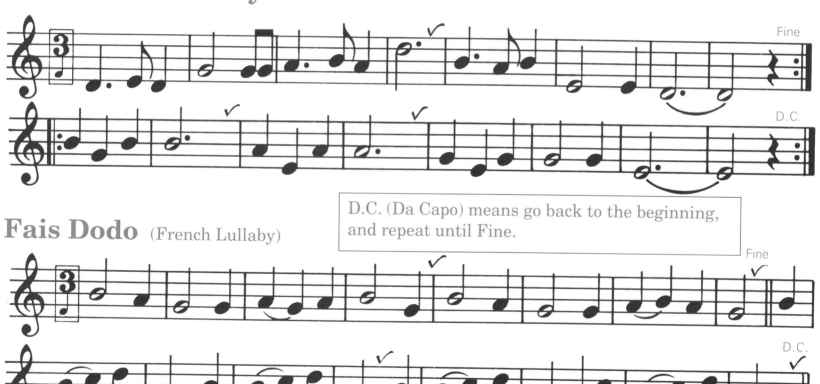

D.C. (Da Capo) means go back to the beginning, and repeat until Fine.

Fais Dodo (French Lullaby)

Rhythm Game

Here are some parts out of the tunes on page 4.
See if you can play them one at a time.
All have 3 counts in each bar.

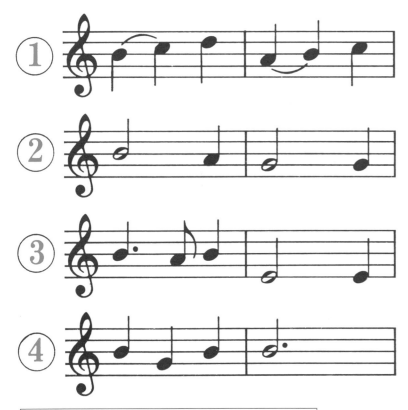

For extra tunes and a duet using the notes and rhythms met so far, see 'Recorder from the Beginning' Tune Book 2, pages 4 to 7.

Now play the game with some friends.
Cover up **numbers 3** and **4** before you begin.
Play either **number 1** or **number 2**.
See if your friends can guess which one you played.
Then let someone else play one, and you all guess again.

Later use **numbers 3** and **4** instead.
Cover up **1** and **2**.
Make the game harder: cover up **number 1**
or **4** only. Choose from the other three!

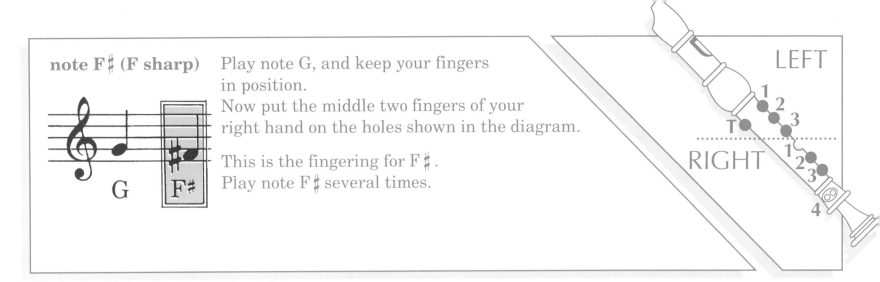

note F♯ (F sharp)

Play note G, and keep your fingers in position.
Now put the middle two fingers of your right hand on the holes shown in the diagram.

This is the fingering for F♯.
Play note F♯ several times.

G   F♯

LEFT

RIGHT

Notice the sharp sign ♯ in front of the note.
This makes it a special note. Later we will
learn to play F natural, which uses different fingering.

Zulu Lullaby

Some tunes use note F♯ (F sharp) instead of note F all the way through. Then, instead of writing the sharp sign (♯) in front of each note F, we place it at the beginning of the stave on the top line, which is also note F.

This turns every F into F♯, including those written in the bottom space.

Sharp (♯) or flat (♭) signs placed at the beginning of a stave are called the **Key Signature**.

Sinner Man

Oh, sinner man, where you gon-na run to? Oh, sinner man, where you gon-na run to?

Oh, sin-ner man, where you gon-na run to? All on that day ———.

Tallis's Canon begins at the end of a bar.

Count 1–2–3 and start to play on count 4.
When you know the tune well, play it as a proper Canon.

Divide into two groups.
Group 1 begins.
When they reach letter A on the music,
Group 2 begins playing from the beginning.

Cradle Song

This tune begins at the end of a bar.
Count 1–2 and play on count 3.
Notice the sharp sign.

Winter Journey

Take special care with
the slurs ⌣ in this piece.

Time Signatures

The number on the stave just before the first note of a tune is called the Time Signature.

This tells us how many "conductor's beats" there are in each bar.
If we do as the Time Signature tells us, we can conduct the band for any tune.

Try to "conduct" a tune whilst someone plays it.
First practise your conducting using the shapes given here.
Count the beats as you conduct them.

When you are ready, turn back to the full tune.
Always count and conduct for one bar before the players join in.
This helps them to begin together.
Use a pencil for a baton!

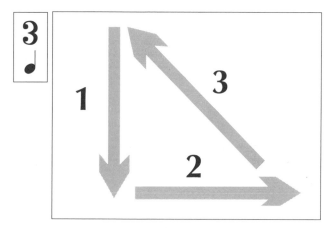

Sinner Man (Page 7)

Oh, sinner   man, where you gon-na run   to?

Fais Dodo (Page 4)

Pokare Kare
Maori song

This song is about some Maoris who are on a hunting trip, away from their families.

The tune and descant both use exactly the same rhythm. When you are playing in two parts, always listen carefully.

Are you playing in time together?
Is your part louder than the other?
It shouldn't be!

Descant

11

More about **Time Signatures**

The shape for conducting four beats in a bar is hard to remember.
Think of a sailing ship.

1	Down	(down the mast)
2	Back	(to the back of the boat)
3	Front	(to the front of the boat)
4	Up	(up the sail)

Count four beats in a bar and practise conducting this shape.

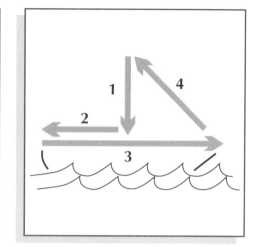

Later you can take turns to conduct "Good King Wenceslas", whilst others play the tune.
Take care to keep conducting and counting during the long notes.

Good King Wenceslas

Another tune to play and then conduct.
Remember the Time Signature tells us how many
conductor's beats there are in each full bar, not
how many notes there are.

For extra tunes and a duet using the notes and
rhythms met so far, see 'Recorder from the
Beginning' Tune Book 2, pages 8 to 11.

Down in Bethlehem

© JH

(Verse)   Little   baby wrapped in white, Sleeping in the candle light,   Mary watching thro' the night, Down in Bethlehem.

(Chorus) Far   a—way,   Far   a—way,   Jesus   came to earth   on   Christ-mas Day.

Not all tunes start on the strong beat
at the beginning of a bar.
Some start on a weak beat at the end
of a bar. This is called an **anacrusis**.

Then we must count the rest of the bar
before we begin.
Turn back and play these tunes again,
counting the beats before you begin.

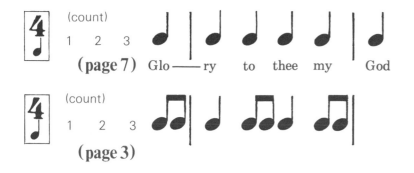

13

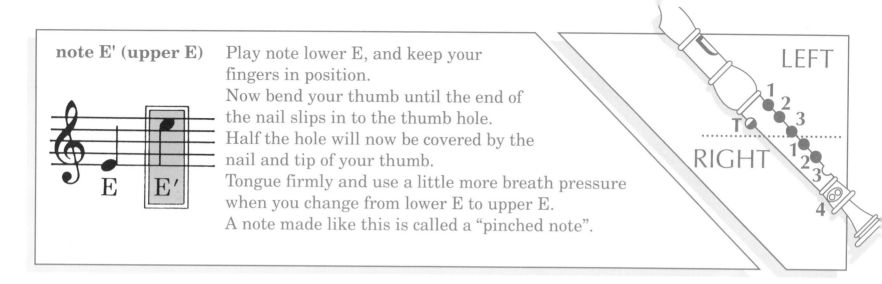

note E' (upper E) Play note lower E, and keep your fingers in position.
Now bend your thumb until the end of the nail slips in to the thumb hole.
Half the hole will now be covered by the nail and tip of your thumb.
Tongue firmly and use a little more breath pressure when you change from lower E to upper E.
A note made like this is called a "pinched note".

E   E'

LEFT

RIGHT

Before learning the tune, practise playing from E' to D'.
Where is this used in the tune?

Old Abram Brown

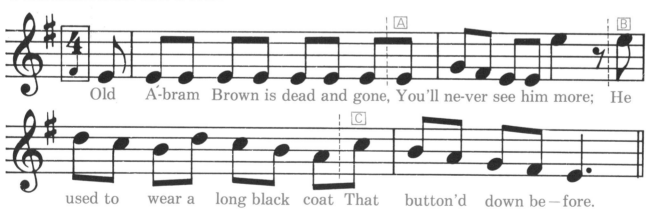

Old   A-bram Brown is dead and gone, You'll ne-ver see him more; He
used to   wear a   long black coat That   button'd   down be—fore.

This is a **round** that will fit in two, three or four parts.
Letters A, B and C show where the starting points are.

14

My Bonnie lies over the ocean

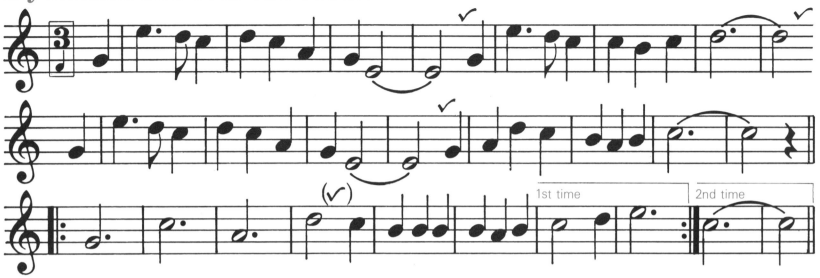

French Carol

For eight duets and some carols using the notes and rhythms met so far, see 'Recorder from the Beginning' Tune Book 2, pages 12 to 20.

An optional second part is given to accompany the chorus. The **tune** notes have stems up (♩) and the **accompaniment** notes have stems down (♩).

15

Now all the forests are at rest (Old German hymn)

In the next tune, notice how the first two bars of lines 1 and 2 are the same.

Is the second half of line 2 used anywhere else?

Remember that a dot above or below a note makes the note **staccato**, or cut off short.

To play staccato say 'tut'.

When you play the tune, be careful to tongue the staccato and slurred notes correctly.

The Lord Mayor's Parade

©JCP

The next song uses two new rhythm patterns,  and
First, say the words and clap the rhythms of (a) and (b).

(a)

That is what I heard her say

(b)

Grandma Grunts said a curious thing

In line (b) two **semi-quavers**
or sixteenth notes
take the place of one **quaver**
or eighth note

Grandma Grunts

Grand-ma Grunts said a curious thing, "Boys may whistle but girls must sing".

That is what I heard her say, 'Twas no longer than yest–er–day.

Boys can whistle, (whistle) Girls must sing tra-la — la — la — la.

Skip to my Lou

Lou,   lou,   skip   to my lou,   Lou,   lou,   skip   to my lou,

Lou,   lou,   skip   to my lou,   skip to my   lou   my   dar——ling.

The next tune (on page 20) uses two new rhythms, ♪♪♪♪ and ♩. ♪
Can you find them in the tune? (Turn over to look, then read on here.)
See how four semiquavers (sixteenth notes) take the time of the first crotchet (quarter note) beat.
Try to clap all the first bar as you say the words.

Here is an exercise to help you learn the other new rhythm.

First play this: (a)

Play again but hold on the tied note: (b)

Here is another way to write (b).
The dot after a note makes the note half as
long again, so (b) and (c) should sound   (c)
exactly the same.

Little Red Wagon

Riding up and down in the little red wag-on, Riding up and down in the little red wag-on,

Riding up and down in the little red wag-on, Won't you be my dar———ling?

Class Activity

Now you can have some fun!
The tunes of 'Skip to my Lou' and 'Little Red Wagon' will fit
together. Split up into two groups and try to play both tunes at
the same time!
Someone must count 1–2 so that you all begin together.

Singers

A group of singers can perform one tune whilst recorders play
the other tune. Then change over.

The Teacher's Book has suggestions for an easy accompaniment
that will fit either tune or both tunes together. Or you can use
the cassette accompaniment.

Both these tunes begin with the end of a bar.
Count 1–2 and play on count 3.

Kum ba ya

Kum ba ya my Lord, Kum ba ya —, Kum ba ya my Lord, Kum ba ya,

Kum ba ya my Lord, Kum ba ya, O Lord —— Kum ba ya.

Clementine

In a ca—vern, in a can—yon, Ex—ca—vat ——ing for a mine,

Lived a min—er, for—ty nin——er, And his daugh——ter Clem-en—tine.

Chorus (same tune)
Oh, my darling, Oh, my darling,
Oh, my darling Clementine!
You are lost and gone forever,
Dreadful sorry, Clementine.

Anacrusis
An incomplete bar at the beginning of a tune is called an **anacrusis**. Then the music starts on a weak beat instead of a strong one. Notice that the last bar of the tune is also incomplete. Add this to the anacrusis and it makes a full bar.

21

More tunes that use E' (upper E)
Ten Green Bottles

For a duet and an extra tune see 'Recorder from the Beginning' Tune Book 2, page 21.

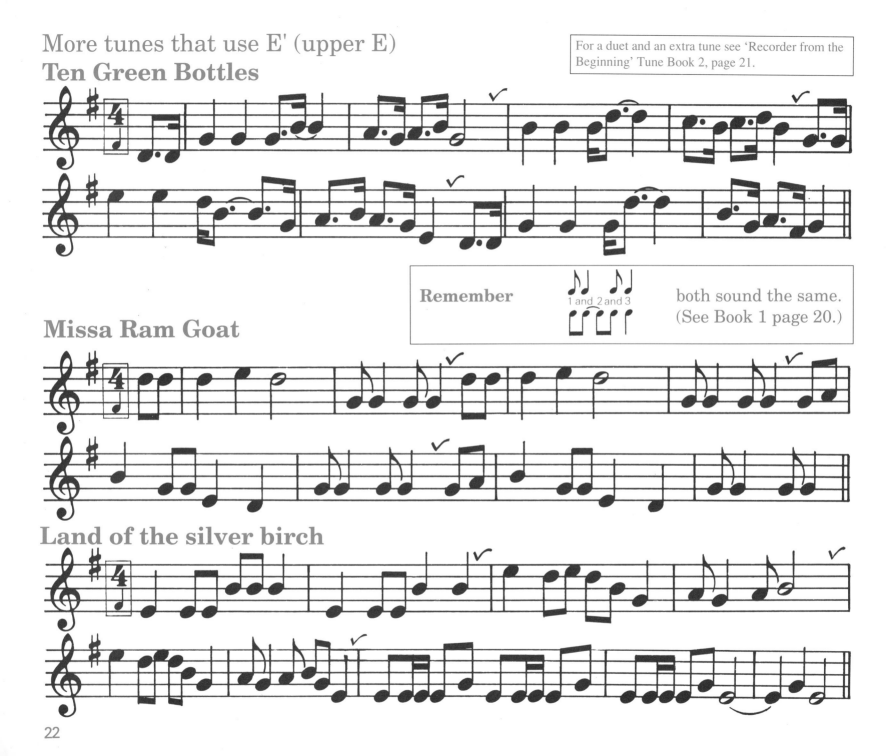

Remember 1 and 2 and 3 both sound the same. (See Book 1 page 20.)

Missa Ram Goat

Land of the silver birch

Kalinka

Cossack Dance

is a minim (half note) rest worth two beats.

©JCP

23

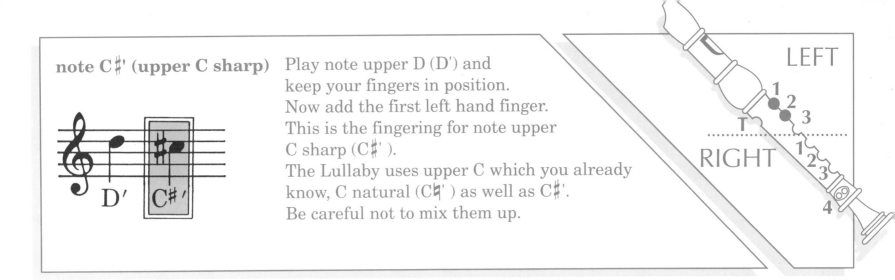

note C♯' (upper C sharp)

Play note upper D (D') and keep your fingers in position. Now add the first left hand finger. This is the fingering for note upper C sharp (C♯'). The Lullaby uses upper C which you already know, C natural (C♮') as well as C♯'. Be careful not to mix them up.

Manx Lullaby

Before you play "Vilikins", practise these bars taken from the tune.

Vilikins and his Dinah

The Banks of Sacramento

Ho, boys, ho ——! For Ca —— li-for —— nia, O! There's
plenty of gold, so I've been told, On the banks of Sa —— cra —— men- to.

25

For two duets and extra tunes see 'Recorder from the Beginning' Tune Book 2, pages 22 to 25.

Class Activity

Kookaburra is a **round** that will fit in two, three or four parts.
You can use **singers** and an **ostinato** as explained on page 3.

Kook a bur ra sits in an old gum tree, Merry merry king of the bush is he-

Laugh Kook a bur ra, Laugh Kook a bur ra, Gay your life will be —————

Tzena has an optional second part to accompany the chorus.
The chorus tune has stems up, the accompaniment tune has stems down.

Chorus

26

A **Mazurka** is a Polish dance,
usually in three sections.
The beginning and end are the same, so we
have used the D.C. sign to tell you when to
go back to the beginning.
Take care to play the slurs properly.

Mazurka

The words of this rhyme will help you to learn some new rhythm patterns that skip along. Say and clap the words, then play the tune.

Incey Wincey Spider

In — cey win — cey spi — der Climb-ing up the wat—er spout.

Down came the rain And washed the spi — der out.

Out came the sun And dried up all the rain, So

In — cey win — cey spi — der Climbed the spout a — gain.

London Bridge

Say and clap, then play. Take care with the quicker notes ♪♪♪ in bar 3 and bar 6.

Lon don Bridge is brok —en down, Dance over my Lad —y Lee.

Lon —don Bridge is brok ——en down, With a gay Lad ———y.

Skipping for fun

In the last two tunes you played
all the rhythms you need in this tune.

Haul Away Joe (Shanty)

So far all the skipping rhythms we have met have been fast, like "Haul Away Joe".
The words helped us to fit in the notes, or we used two big counts in each bar.
Slower skipping tunes use six little counts in each bar, grouped in threes: ♫♫ ♫♫
The Time Signature will be $\frac{6}{8}$

See how the notes can fit together. Count and clap each line.

Use 1 count for ♪

Use 2 counts for ♩ (= ♫)

Use 3 counts for ♩. (= ♫♫ or ♩♪)

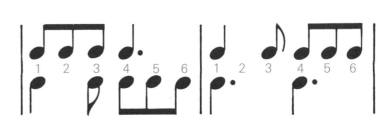

Count and clap each tune before you play it.

What would you do?

© JCP (Tune)

For extra tunes using these rhythms see 'Recorder from the Beginning' Tune Book 2, pages 26 and 27.

What would you do if you had a cow, Who
nev—er said 'Moo' but pre——ferred a 'Bow-wow'. Who
played the guit—ar and lived in a stye, And
put on gol—osh—es to keep her feet dry?

Row, Row, Row your boat (Round) Ideas for **Class Activity** are on page 3.

Row, row, row your boat, Gent—ly down the stream———,
Merr-i-ly, merr-i-ly, merr-i-ly, merr-i-ly, Life is such a dream———.

31

The first Nowell (Includes C#')

For more carols, including duets, see 'Recorder from the Beginning' Tune Book 2, pages 14 to 17.

God rest you merry, Gentlemen (Includes E')

Unto us a boy is born

The Child's Carol

A Child this day is born

Repeat for Chorus

33

The **Tango** is a dance from Argentina,
a country in South America.
A Tango always uses the rhythm ♩. ♪♩♩
How many times is this rhythm used in the
dance tune here?
Look out for the Upper Es and C sharps.

Tango   Not too fast

For six more duets see 'Recorder from the Beginning'
Tune Book 2, pages 18 to 21 and 23 to 24.

Learn to play the tune first.
Then learn the accompaniment.
Later, you and a friend can play both
parts at once. You can also play along
with the cassette accompaniment.

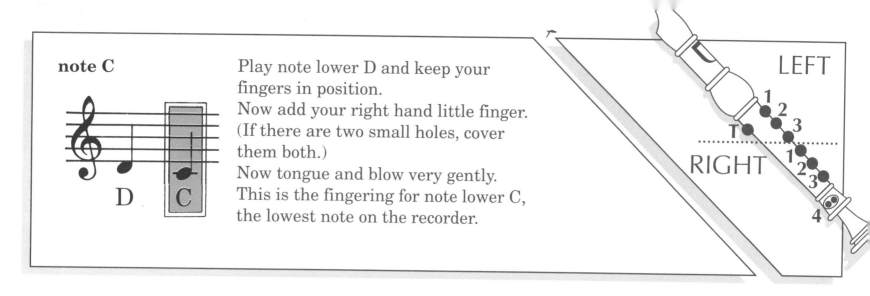

note C

Play note lower D and keep your fingers in position.
Now add your right hand little finger. (If there are two small holes, cover them both.)
Now tongue and blow very gently.
This is the fingering for note lower C, the lowest note on the recorder.

All the holes on your recorder should be covered. If the note doesn't sound correctly, make sure all your fingers are flat and covering the holes.
Tongue and blow very gently.

Barnyard Song
Practise the last bar of the first line before you play the tune.

I had a cat and the cat pleased me, I fed my cat by yon-der tree.

verse 1
Cat goes fiddle—i——dee.

verses 2 – 3
Hen goes chinny chuck, Cat goes fiddle–i——dee.
Duck goes quack quack,

Here are two more tunes which use lower C.

The fireman's not for me

Old Joe Clark

Old Joe Clark he had a mule, his name was Mor-gan Brown. And ev-'ry tooth in

Morgan's head was six-teen in-ches round. Fare you well, old Joe Clark,

Fare you well, I say. Fare you well, Old Joe Clark, for I am going a-way.

Class Activity

Both halves of this tune can be played or sung at the same time. So when you know the tune well, split into two groups.

Singers can be Group 1. They start at A.

Recorders can be Group 2. They start at B.

When Group 2 reach the end they go straight back to A and play up to B again.

Both groups should finish together.

Hollow elm tree

Count 1 – 2 – 3 and play on count 4.

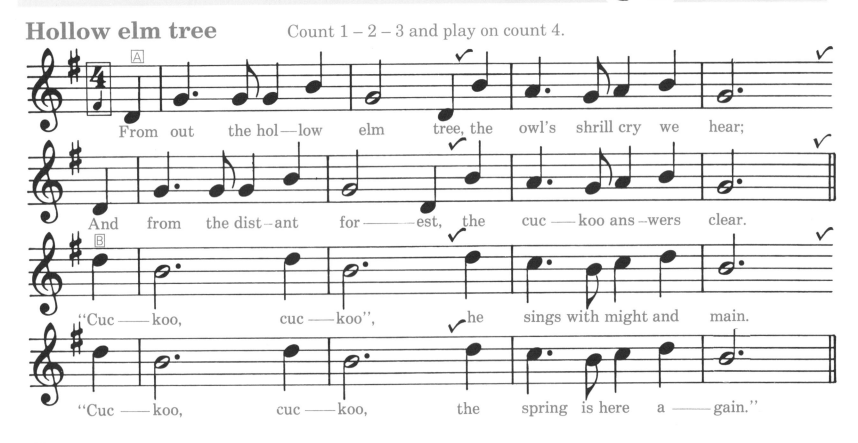

From out the hol—low elm tree, the owl's shrill cry we hear;

And from the dist–ant for———est, the cuc———koo ans–wers clear.

"Cuc———koo, cuc———koo", he sings with might and main.

"Cuc———koo, cuc———koo, the spring is here a———gain."

Li'l Liza Jane

I know a girl that you don't know, Li'l Li — za Jane,

Way down South in Bal — ti — mo', Li'l Li — za Jane.

Oh, E — li — za, li'l Li — za Jane,

Oh, E — li — za, li'l Li — za Jane.

Class Activity

When you can play the song well, you can add two **ostinato** accompaniments. They are made from parts of the tune marked A and B.

You can use xylophone, chime bars or recorders.

Only use ostinato A to begin with.

Play A twice before the tune joins in.
Later, try using ostinato B instead.

To use both ostinato parts together, start like a round. Begin with ostinato A.
Then ostinato B joins in.
Both keep playing, then **singers** and/or **recorders** join in with the main tune.

Both these tunes have an **anacrusis**.
They begin with the end of a bar.
Count 1 2 3 4 5 and begin on count 6.
Notice how the first and last bars add together to make one full bar.

It's raining, it's pouring Can you play the second line in one breath?

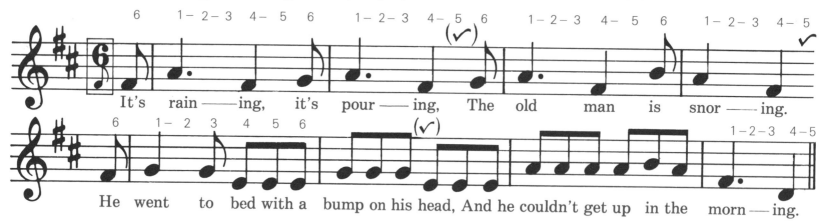

It's rain——ing, it's pour——ing, The old man is snor——ing.

He went to bed with a bump on his head, And he couldn't get up in the morn——ing.

There was a young farmer of Leeds

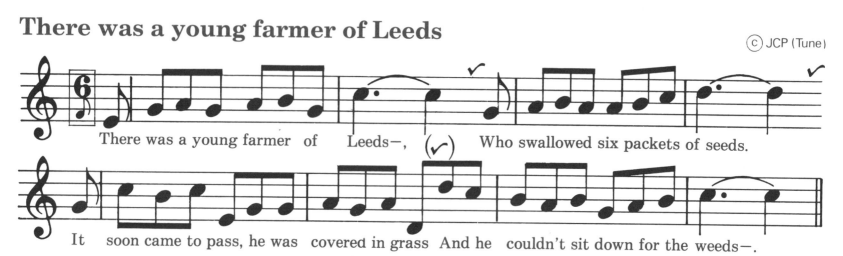

There was a young farmer of Leeds—, Who swallowed six packets of seeds.

It soon came to pass, he was covered in grass And he couldn't sit down for the weeds—.

Scarborough Fair (Includes C♯′ and E′)

One More River (Includes E′)

More use of notes lower C and upper E.

Old Paint

For more tunes using lower C and upper E see 'Recorder from the Beginning' Tune Book 2, pages 28 to 29.

Good — bye   Old   Paint,   I'm a   leav — ing   Chey — enne.

My   foot's   in the   stirrup,   my   po — ny   won't   stand.

I'm   off   to Mon — tan — a,   I'm   leav — ing   Chey — enne.

Shule Agra

Botany Bay
The verse and chorus both use the same tune.

Class Activity see page 3 for help in using singers and players.

I like the flowers Round in 2, 3 or 4 parts

I like the flow—ers, I like the daff—o–dils, I like the moun-tains,

I like the roll-ing hills. I like the fire——side, when all the lamps are low,

(Last time only)

Boom-ter-arr-ah, boom-ter-arr-ah, boom-ter-arr-ah, boom-ter-arr-ah, Boom!

43

Mango Walk

This tune usually has a **Rumba** accompaniment.
Ask a friend to play the maracas,
using this word pattern to keep the rhythm.

Later, someone else can add claves (or a wooden block,
or rhythm sticks). Count 8 quaver beats in each bar,
and tap on counts ①, ④ and ⑦.

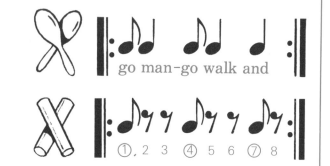

go man-go walk and

① 2 3 ④ 5 6 ⑦ 8

Concert Beguine (Quite slowly)

The **Beguine** is a dance from South America. It combines two rhythms. Ask a friend to clap the first rhythm or play it on claves while you play the tune.

Your friend should play the pattern twice as an introduction before you begin. Count the beats aloud. Later another friend can play the second rhythm, using a tambourine. Count aloud and only tap each time you say "and".

To play both rhythms at once, Player 1 begins and after two bars Player 2 joins in. After two more bars the recorders begin the tune.

1 — 2 3 4

1 and 2 and 3 and 4 and

Tune writing using notes we know

C D E F# G A B C' C#' D' E'

See if you can make up some music to finish off the tune on the next page.
Follow the instructions carefully.

A Say and clap line 1, then play it.

B Say the words and clap the rhythm of the first half of line 2.
Now make up some tune on your recorder to fit the words you clapped.
Begin on the notes given.
Keep trying until you like your tune, then write it down.
Now do the same thing again to complete the second line.
End the line on one of the four notes given.

C Make up line 3 in the same way.
Say and clap the words first.

D Play the last line. Keep trying different notes to fill in the empty bar until you like the tune.
Then write down the notes.

Two little monkeys

For more tune writing see 'Recorder from the Beginning' Tune Book 2, pages 30 to 31.

Contents

Printed in Singapore by Kyodo Printing Co. (S'pore) Pte Ltd